Light
in
Slow
Motion

Light
in
Slow
Motion

Keith Wrassmann

AVAILABLE LIGHT PRESS
Maineville, Ohio

Printed in the United States of America.

ISBN: 978-1-961631-03-8
ISBN: 978-1-961631-04-5 (ebook)

Library of Congress Control Number: 2024950621

First Edition

Published by Available Light Press, Maineville, Ohio.

www.availablelightpress.com

Visit the author's website at www.keithwrassmann.com

For my mother,
who walks with the grace of the light.

Contents

You are in the world
where the golden light has dimmed,
where all remembrance of who you are
has faded to the blackness of new night.
But this is not a darkness without sight,
for light is light
even in its slowest hue.

Light
in
Slow
Motion

Sight

Dear Soul,
when you are ready,
lift your face.
The pathway you travel
may block the sun,
but you are not destined
to walk among shadows.
The light in loss will lead you through the dark.
Worry, fear, and uncertainty
are momentary phantoms
that disappear when you have seen through them.
They are not permanent.
A brightness in the distance remains.
It calls you to move forward.
It reminds you hope exists,
a provision for the journey
when all other light has dimmed.
The eyes of your heart
can view the full spectrum of life,
and see through death,
to find that what you've lost
is not lost,
but has changed frequency
in passing from the realm of human sight.

Slow Light

Nature's way
is to show in one hand
the breathtaking blue of the butterfly wing,
the ocean depth,
the infinite sky,
and then present in the other hand
the deterioration of all things in the world,
in time, in humanity.
Do not mistake either hand
for the sovereignty of God,
for nature has no such justice,
but governs by a predetermined law.
It cannot change its mind
or choose to remove its terror.
You are merely passing through,
and this by choice.
You are subject to its bounds
for only a little while.
It is not your true home.
It is an illusion through which you move—
light in slow motion—
to thrill and traumatize you,
to fascinate and frighten you,
to enlighten and burden you,
to offer the experience
of what you cannot have in faster light.

Granite

You are in the world
where the golden light has dimmed,
where all remembrance of who you are
has faded to the blackness of new night—
the journey through a darkness
unimaginable until you saw it for yourself.
But this is not a darkness without sight,
for light is light
even in its slowest hue.
And on the way,
your eyes inevitably adjust
and see what you could not detect before,
like waking from a dream
where you were lost,
and awareness rushes back to you.
You are not lost.
You sojourn through a black granite world
that sparkles depending on
how you hold it to the light—
the focused light of your eyes
which reveals its true essence.
This world is what you think it is,
and what you do not think it is.
Glory is in the unveiling,

in the rebirth of the self,
in the renewal of discovery,
in the remembrance of
the momentary nature of this light.

Impending

We learn from what we lose,
regardless of the severity.
Such lessons are the reason for slow light
that binds and loosens,
that hurts and heals.
Only in certain darkness
can we perceive a limitation,
our finite self,
the purpose only for a brief time,
with a beginning and an ending.
This light in which we live
is a work of mastery
with nothing left to chance
but what we forgot we wanted.
Loss teaches us
what we could not understand
from the perspective of everlasting light,
our feet on the edge of the golden shore,
looking out over the dark expanse.

Dichotomy

You looked but never found.
Such is the way of life
in a world of infinite potential,
the only guarantee being your experience.
All of life is a yearning
for what lies outside your reach.
You imagined what would make you happy,
then tried to grasp it.
The light here is arrayed in a way
to give you opportunity to create and fulfill,
desire and achieve.
But it also allows for the imperfect,
the incomplete,
and the deprivation.
How you handle disappointment is what matters.
The fear of survival tells you
only reception of desire has value.
But you know better.
You know that wisdom reveals itself best
in the darkest moment,
the moment you did not think you could go on,
but did.

Undoing

May you find comfort
when you cannot see
the reason for why it happened,
and what it took away.
May you find wellness
when you do not understand
the feelings you have
that whisper *you should have done more.*
May you find strength
when you are at the edge
of what you think you can endure,
that you cannot continue.
You will go on.
This darkness is a necessary part
of a journey to the center of the undoing,
and it is here where you wrestle with
the lessening,
the falling away,
and the leaving.
The evening is the time for letting go.
The night is for remembering and processing.
The morning is for welcoming back the light.

There

You can move forward,
regardless of what you have endured.
Hopelessness and depression
have no rightful ownership of you,
for you belong to the light,
and are light.
Such dimness is a momentary pause
on the road to a destination
so glorious
you would not believe it
while on the way.
The path is before you,
so walk,
for it is yours to claim
regardless of what may block it.
You can overcome,
for it is your right of existence,
even if you've lost the golden light,
for it is there,
it is always there.

Fulfillment

You wanted to find fulfillment in the end,
for it is at the end
where all your life unfolds before your view:
happiness, sadness,
success, failure,
your impact on others
a ripple in the fabric of space-time,
with each soul connected
in the invisible realm of light.
Fulfillment is in the living,
in each moment that passes,
regardless of its outcome
or how you wished it would have gone.
The light here is slow enough to let you
grieve, rejoice,
struggle, achieve.
Experience will blur into your very being,
and this is your learning,
your growth,
your gain,
the worth of your endeavor
in navigating the darkness
where even the bravest angels fear to watch.

Progression

When the emotional toll is too much,
and waves of
sadness
anger
longing
crash on the shore of your soul,
time will take your hand
and slowly lead you back to safer ground.
From here, you will gain perspective
on all that has come to pass.
Time looks backwards and forwards
to show you what you need to see.
Nothing is lost or forgotten.
Time ever moves into newness,
one moment leading to another,
an endless progression
that enables the soul to learn,
to feel, to process,
to change, to heal.
In time, the sea will calm,
and you will return to the shore
with eyes reborn,
to see again the beauty
where sky meets water.

Self-Worth

You thought you were finished
because of what happened.
It was out of your control.
And who will love me now? you asked.
All your life,
you looked for the thing that would
sustain you,
fulfill you,
make you whole.
You sought worth from without,
an exterior catalyst
to prove to you that what was within
was good enough,
valuable,
deserving.
It's not until you fall that you can see.
Truth presents itself in the rebuilding,
for it is here
that you examine the pieces,
realign them,
understand them,
put them where they belong.
And what emerges is the realization
that your worth

does not depend on others' judgment,
or acceptance,
or acknowledgment,
for you are the image of an eternal essence,
an expression of a never-ending light,
brilliance in the courage of your coming forth.

Memory

You were not ready for change.
No one ever is.
And now, let autumn
rush and flash
with the magnificence of its ending,
moving so fast
you cannot stop it,
though you want to.
You long to savor
what you know cannot last,
to experience light
as long as it shines.
But this is a light that cannot be put out.
It does not pass from existence,
but transforms
through the illusion of departure.
It travels to the place where human eyes
fail to see.
The memory of light
is a gift of sight,
that though it may dim with years,
it never disappears.
You may forever carry its essence,
because it is a part of you.

Shift

Pursue peace,
for what is the advantage of discontent?
Though the trials of life
may upset you,
the path to contentment
is always open.
Which way will you direct your heart?
If you fear letting go of turmoil,
that it would mean you have lost,
the only true loss is holding on to disquiet.
Letting go is a victory
only the angry can understand.
It is the blessing of movement
from one place to another—
where once there was only darkness,
now there is unconstrained light,
renewed perspective,
and the hope of seeing face to face,
to see again the beauty in another.

The Forgetting

Remember today
that the pain you feel
from some unrequited sentiment
or anguish of unmet longing
is a sensation in a reality
that is not your inherent dwelling place.
This is not your natural state of being.
Nor is it your one chance
to get everything right.
In the forgetting,
you lose the sense of oneness with the light
and move through dim spaces
you could not imagine
when dreaming of the depth of life
and what it could be.
The forgetting is a blessing
that reveals the unexpected,
that gives you what you did not know you needed.
You are lost, but not lost.
You lack, but are still whole.
You are alone, but not forsaken.
The path you travel winds to the left and right.
The purpose of such hardship is your gain.
You are forever loved
in the golden realm of light.

Dawn

It was survival mode.
You did the best you could,
given the circumstances.
But now, you do not have to carry
guilt and shame;
you can learn to deal with
the roots of why they linger.
You cannot go back
and undo the trauma.
Healing does not require
that you reverse all that happened,
but that you process the
thoughts
feelings
emotions
of what remains.
The past holds fear
that keeps you from looking,
from facing what you never thought you could.
But you do not belong to the past.
You belong to the now,
where you move and breathe
with the newness each morning brings,
with the ability to see through what was,

what happened, and why,
and to clear away the dim hues,
as you will,
and as you must,
for it is your nature to return to wholeness
as darkness must give way to burgeoning light.

Treasure

I remember you.
I will speak to you
when you have no one
to turn to.
You might not hear my voice,
but you will know
I am here.
The subtlety of the moment
will remind you
of a faraway light
you cannot remember,
though you have tried.
This life is not for the remembering,
but for the forgetting.
And this is why loss
moves in the silence of shadow,
and why it leaves such heartache in its wake.
Human nature only knows what it sees.
But I am keeping record
of everything that has come to pass.
And when you cannot bear the moment,
I remember you—
in your journey through depth and shallow,
in your going out and coming back.
I remember you.

Last Day

If this were your last day,
what would you think
of your life?
Would you wish you would have done
what you were scared to try?
Would you harbor regret for
missed opportunities,
unfulfilled desires,
broken relationships?
How would you view
loss,
tragedy,
loneliness,
or suffering?
Would you sit in bitterness from them
or find contentment in
what they taught you?
And what about love?
Would you wish
you would have given it more freely,
or received it more sincerely?
It is human to think such things.
It is human to judge yourself
based on your expectations.

But under the pressure of survival,
just to live is a triumph.
Experience is its own reward.
The meaning you attribute to your life
is not universal.
Meaning is for you alone
to make sense of your journey.
You live even after the end.
Experience will continue
until you have accomplished everything,
and then the void will expand,
and the creation will renew.

Relinquish

The great light will never fade,
no matter how hard you rage against it
when life does not go as you want.
The sting of dissatisfaction
can push you to
think,
say,
and do
the previously unimaginable.
But this life is not meant for flawless living,
but for the mistakes
that make you perfect in the end.
Frustration and anger will pass,
and you will not remember
what upset you so much.
Release anger,
forgive others,
forgive yourself.

Opportunity

Struggle and hardship bring opportunity.
How will you grow?
What will you learn?
How would you become stronger
in the absence of obstacle?
Perspective changes
when you allow yourself
to undergo the process.
Understanding changes
when you walk through
what feels insurmountable.
To know is to experience.
We assign meaning to feelings
and then let them dictate self-image.
But feelings are the way we process the impact;
they do not exist
to trap you in joy or terror,
or to define you.
The beauty in opportunity
is the chance for expansion,
to move you from one place to another,
to fulfill the purpose
of why you live in flesh.

Cycle

Not ready for winter,
you were unwilling to let go
of the one who warmed your face,
who comforted you
with the peace of love.
He lingered as long as he could,
like the tree that longs
to keep its leaves
even though the season is changing.
All of life is a never-ending cycle—
ending and beginning,
declining and renewing,
death and rebirth.
You will come through.
You will pass this time
experiencing the intimacy of sorrow,
knowing and processing
what it means to lose.
But you will find light in loss.
And when you have woven
through the depth
of this new uncertainty,
you will emerge
to look upon the world with understanding,

not forgetting the past,
but moving forward with the wisdom
loss brings,
that the sun rises again.

Solitary Light

It wasn't for nothing.
You know this.
But the pain
says otherwise.
Clouds of insecurity
block the light
from reaching your eyes.
You are passing through the nether realm
where future sight and memory collide.
But this is a momentary step
on the journey of life.
What is the purpose?
How do I continue?
Such questions of travel
are necessary for processing
what is,
what was,
what will be.
In time, the clouds will dissipate
as darkness fades to solitary light.
And in this light,
you will pass the boundary of fear
and find again the hope of living.

Departing Light

Would you have known
what it means to be human
without the experience of separation?
This life in flesh
is a temporary flash
of majesty and torment,
an opportunity to see and to feel,
to love and to lose.
It's the losing we struggle with.
We do not understand departures.
They go against our knowledge of the truth—
that life should ever end,
that life could ever end.
But what if you could see departing light?
What if you could lift the veil
and for one moment
glimpse what lies beyond our mortal bounds?
Love is never lost;
it only transforms from one expression to another.
The soul will find its way back to the light.
This is its victory.

Healing

Healing is remembering who you are
and what you are a part of.
It is only when you have had enough
that you look for an answer.
The light hides itself
beneath the guise of what your hands can touch.
You cannot see it with your human eyes.
It is the you
who now must learn to mend.
Trauma fragments the soul
in bits and pieces sharp like shattered glass,
so its reflection is no longer singular,
but multi-faceted and disassociated.
From here, you cannot see yourself as whole.
But this is where recovery begins.
The soul must fracture
to learn the lessons of what it means to live.
Experience defines purpose.
The journey back to singularity
is the path of healing,
of growing,
of gaining,
of moving on.

Inextinguishable

You lost track of the light in him,
like when a candle flame
wanes at the end of its wax
and slowly vanishes.
And who can bring it back?
The fading was the hardest part.
And the finality of disappearance
was a shock that shook you to your human core.
You still saw him in dreams,
a visitation from the realm of sleep,
but morning light
brought back the reality
of physical sight.
It was then that you knew
this world is but a shadow of the truth
that bends and presses light into slow hues,
that it may offer fear in its dim hand.
But life belongs to you,
for life is what you are.
Although the fading is the hardest part,
the light of life is
inextinguishable.

Mirage

Deal with it.
Do not let it
paralyze your forward moving thoughts.
This obstacle may intimidate you,
but you are not enslaved
to the power you have given it.
What exterior mirage
is greater than the light inside your soul?
It is human to protect yourself
by avoiding conflict.
But expansion comes through purposed confrontation.
Do not ruminate on
what you cannot reverse.
Instead, decide you will not rest until
you traverse this outer darkness.
Shadows fade
in the illumination of light.

Bitterness

Bitterness will show you
what you still have to
acknowledge,
process,
incorporate,
and accept.
It is a mirror you do not need to
stand in front of
in order to see into your soul.
The unmistakable feelings
reflect
the situation that troubles you,
that will not subside regardless of
how you hold it up against the light.
Awareness is necessary
so you may find the way to overcome.
The root may take the form of
unmet desire,
unfairness,
pain,
hurt,
or loss.
Whether the offense is justified or not
makes no difference,

for you received it as you did,
and you cannot go back in time
to change it.
The resolution hides in understanding.
Look inside yourself
to scatter gathered darkness.
Find the way forward.
You have the power
to calm the inner storm.
The decision of acceptance is your peace.

Move

Return
from where you were,
from what you said,
from what you did.
Life is not limited
by past endeavors,
but ever expands
into the newness of each moment.
The present is the future come to pass.
Shadows are dependent on blocked light.
So move.
Walk into the morning
where the dew turns the grass emerald green,
glistening with new sunlight,
the expectation of the coming day,
where possibility finds fulfillment.

Darkness

Even the darkness is light.
It's just that you've been here
so long
you don't notice anymore.
But you knew this would happen.
You knew you would forget
for your own benefit.
You knew one day
you would look into the depth
of the blackest black
and think it was really black,
unable to discern the beauty
of this master stroke.
The darkness hides the reason you are here.
The mask of fear obscures your common sight.
You think you are alone.
You think you are separate from
that in which you are immersed.
But even the darkness is light.

Boundary

You held on
as long as you could
before you had to let go.
It wasn't the letting go
that was difficult,
but the holding on.
Life convinces us
that what we grasp
is indispensable,
whether we attain it
by gift or hard work.
Human nature cannot see
farther than its own limitation.
Slow light sets the boundary of sight.
But life does not consist
in what you do or don't have.
It is the experience of the thing
that matters.
Permanence is an illusion.
Duration is measurable
only because it ends.
Repetition gives opportunity
to gain all that the experience offers.
Perspective is the scope that pierces the veil.

Emptiness

The hole forms within
from where you faltered,
or think you did.
It does not depend on your intention,
for consequences come
regardless of the nature
of the action.
But all things heal,
though not at the same speed.
Reminders are an echo of the pain.
To navigate this emptiness
takes courage—
the torch that reveals
the roughness of the walls,
and shows the path
so you may step in hope.
Emptiness is not a final destination,
but a creation of
unmet desire.
The return to wholeness
is in the acceptance of the thing,
and acceptance is the harbinger of peace.

Present Oneness

Why does anything here matter, you asked,
when I and everyone I love
will eventually be gone?
The light replied,
Do not let the temporal nature
of this world
fool you into thinking
it is meaningless.
Life is lived in each moment,
in each breath you take,
in the time you share with one another,
regardless of what seems like a brevity
when someone you love leaves.
No one truly dies.
They just pass from one realm to another,
to their true home,
where memories never fade,
and all that happened builds their present now,
no more past or future,
only the present oneness
of all they are and experienced.

Revealing

You will awaken from this dream
and return to where you started,
though you cannot see that now.
This light that harbors you
also blinds you,
upholding a multi-faceted illusion
so elusive yet beautiful
you cannot discern it
or stop looking.
Light and darkness play upon one another,
creating moments of
happiness and sadness,
joy and sorrow,
to reveal in you slowly
something so ancient
you cannot remember.
Memory of the golden shore
is like a whisper you cannot quite hear,
though you may try.
You will journey through this all-encompassing light,
grasping what it has to offer,
for this was your hope,
your destiny.

Knowing

The light has slowed
enough to notice a difference
from when you began.
The waning is the time for introspection,
for incorporating gain or loss,
pleasure or pain,
joy or sorrow.
No fear exists in dimming light,
but only opportunity
to comprehend the distance you have come.
Human nature longs to know itself,
to explore,
to experience,
to discover what is possible;
it longs to see beyond its limitation
of all it has to learn by doing.
But it is in the doing
that desire transforms into knowing.
Every moment is for you,
whether positive or negative,
to illuminate the soul that hides within,
to understand the truth of who you are.

Interaction

It is time to move forward.
Enough of staying in
one position
where you think you must
examine every moment,
as if to justify
the reason for the way you feel.
Feelings are a reaction to
the way in which you moved,
the way time passed,
the interaction that healed or hurt you.
An experience is momentary.
How you incorporate it into your soul
is what matters most.

Avoidance

Enough of avoiding an opportunity
because you fear you may fail.
Enough of allowing
unknown possibilities
to dictate your actions.
What is failure, anyway?
Is it the final destination,
or merely a stopping point
on the way to bringing
dream into reality?
No one said it would be easy
or free from pain.
Pain can show you
where you need to step next.
Use it to your advantage.
Avoidance is a reflection
of what you are afraid to face.
But you do not have to live like this.
You can choose to move forward
into the newness of desire,
discovering what waits ahead,
rejoicing in the learning,
in overcoming obstacles,
transforming light with your imagination.

Self-Criticism

What do you say to yourself
when you falter
or make a mistake?
We struggle when our human nature
reminds us of its frailty,
its intentional imperfection,
its physical limitations.
We forget the beauty of this creation
that allows us to experience
the full range of possibility,
the high and the low,
the wanted and unwanted.
Perhaps the flaw is not in what was made,
but in our response to it,
in our inability to retain knowledge
of who we are
and why we are here.
We wanted the light slow enough
to explore with fascination
the essence of our being,
in the immersion of limitation,
where faltering and mistakes
help reveal the glory of the soul.
Love transcends all negativity.

Behold

You will go the course you planned
until you finish it,
and whether you enjoy or despise it
is up to you.
Happiness and sadness
do not depend on what comes to pass,
but on how you respond
to the moments of life.
If your response is negative,
you may find a way to see it differently.
Accompanying pain
will try to convince you
no other perspective exists.
But pain is not meant to oppress you,
but to focus you
on navigating how and where to step.
All of life is a longing toward completion,
toward oneness,
a journey without remembrance
of the final destination,
where obstacles litter the path
to build and grow you.
You have the ability
to find the positive or negative,

regardless of emotion,
and behold the light
that ever shines
outside human sight.

Letting Go

When you do not want to let go,
let go.
Can you control the outcome
or manipulate the pieces
to align as you want?
Can you command a situation
to play out according to your plans?
The hand grasps
in the fear of unwanted consequences,
that it may bring about desire.
It is human to strive to prevent
potential loss.
This is the way of things.
But when the soul finally forgoes
insistence on its own way,
it learns to greet the outcome with
humility,
patience,
acceptance,
and confidence that
what has come to pass
is but one moment in time
that builds and moves you farther,
somewhere hopeful,
somewhere brighter.

Magnificent

What you think is lost
is not lost.
The world is arrayed in light
so dense
you cannot see its bounds.
The speed of light creates the present now,
hiding the existence
of a greater reality
your human eyes cannot perceive.
What you do not see seems lost to you,
for you have lost contact,
lost touch.
Yearning can't reverse the disappearance.
But memory stores feelings,
emotions,
moments.
It retains the signature of life—
another's love impressed upon your soul.
The flesh can only hold your being
for what seems like a moment,
for each light must return
to that from which it came,
in its brave and glorious journey,
having undergone something so breathtaking,
something so magnificent.

Secret

Embrace each moment,
even if it hurts.
The multi-colored world was made for you,
even though at times
you may not think so.
Misfortune has a way of telling you
that you are the one to blame,
that it is your fault,
that you deserved it.
Never believe it.
Expand your focus beyond the sole desire
to experience only what seems good,
or what is pleasurable,
or what is for your own happiness.
Move past the association
that all pain is negative,
that all sorrow is bad,
that all wrongs from others' hands
are payment for some failure.
All experience is for your benefit,
moving you where you have not yet been.
Find solace in living,
in the passage of time,
regardless of the outcome,
the secret of the purpose of the soul.

Diamond

Misfortune was your fortune,
but you could not see it.
It was not until hardship came
that darkness brought you light.
You resisted what pressed against you
because you feared being overcome.
But pressure forms diamonds from dust.
In the courage of acceptance,
you opened your fist
to receive the unimaginable.
And then the falling,
like a sinking stone in still water,
the weight taking you where you
never wanted to go.
The bottom was a dark and silent rest—
an inner processing,
a recounting of words, actions, regrets,
a longing for all to be made right,
for understanding,
to be made whole again.
From down there,
the light above was a blurred dimness.
Not until you released the trauma
did it release you,

and you rose again
with treasure in your hand
through clouds that dispersed
like after dropping their rain,
only to reveal the bright blue sky
and the golden sun.

Changing

Do not fear the coming winter,
for when the first snow falls,
you will remember
that what otherwise would have been rain
is now a gently glistening diamond sky,
the world remade,
a reminder that everything changes,
even yourself.
You pass your life
moving from one form to another,
one perspective to another,
one understanding to another—
the progress of the purpose of
what it means to live.
Your path today
may not be the same path tomorrow,
though the destination does not change.
Each moment offers an endless potential
where experience proves the worth of this existence,
this opportunity to laugh and to grieve,
to hurt and to heal.

Continuation

The grief in loss
is the hurt of separation,
the insecurity of solitude,
the longing for the hand.
Light does not know darkness
until it dims itself
enough to notice a change.
And only in the dimming
can it process the depth
of its own awareness.
The light in loss
is the love that remains
through the darkness,
in the soul,
in emotion.
Love overcomes grief,
for it carries with it
the memory of what was—
the pleasure of relationship,
the comfort of union,
the entwining of hands.
It carries the hope of what is to come—
the restoration
of goodness, beauty, warmth—

the illumination of hope realized,
like in the sunrise,
or the return of spring,
when you again see face to face.

Hurt

Hurt left you the option
to hold on to it
or let it go.
Will you live in the recall of trauma
or move beyond it?
Human nature replays the hurt
to remember the feeling,
that it may guard you
from future hurt.
Hurt threatens survival.
Survival is the basis of all fear.
The light in flesh must learn to live with hurt,
to navigate its ability to
paralyze you,
create doubt,
foster insecurity.
You can learn to process all experience,
to recover the ability to move forward,
to transform pain into growth,
and find hope that looks forward
even through the darkest night.

Outer

You were living your life in the dream,
the dream of a reality
you never had reason to question,
until suffering came.
Desperation of life
gave you pause to consider
what you were doing here,
and the nature of this dark world.
But slow light hides the reason for the night,
when day was all you thought you needed,
all you thought you wanted.
Suddenly, this earth was foreign to you,
like an unrecognizable face
or a language you could not understand.
How can I continue? you asked.
The light replied,
I am for you,
and always watch over you
through your high and your low,
always moving you through light and shadow,
for each serves a purpose
in your brave passage,
your endeavor to go out and come back,
to live and to die,
to learn and to love.

Create

You ran
though you did not need to.
The only thing that chased you
was what your own fear conjured,
a ghost that vanished
once you realized its origin.
On the leading edge of slower light,
you have the potential
to bring into existence
what you dread or cherish,
what you fear or love.
The world works for you
even when you think
it works against you.
Benefit exists in both the fortunate
and unfortunate.
You are the author of your life
and have the ability
to paint new scenes with brave or muted hues,
to change the path
to go where you see fit,
each step an unfolding of your passage.

Forgiveness

How many years must pass
before you say
I forgive you?
The living hurt each other
intentionally and unintentionally.
Is this the fault of life here,
or the necessary anguish of living?
Would the light in you desire to dim
the light of another?
Absent of fear,
we desire the best for each other.
The triumph of life
is for light to live in flesh
and surpass its limitation,
to overcome the momentary boundary
of the pull of self-survival.
Void of the flesh,
you loved each other
in the golden realm where light can never dull.
It is only here
that you allow yourself for a brief time
to know and understand pain,
frustration,
what it feels like to yearn

yet not be able to do anything about it,
and to see it through to its end
until you finally can look up again
and say
I forgive you.

Returning

Life pushed you down
as hard and far as it could,
as life does here
in the shadow of the divine,
in the necessity of abandonment.
You searched for wisdom and knowledge
of who you are,
for the whisper never quite vanished
that you were more than what your eyes saw,
or hands touched.
Truth reveals itself in fading light,
for it is in this moment
that all is finally unveiled,
no longer able to maintain the façade
of where it was leading you
or what it meant to show you.
Life is a journey from light to dark,
and back again.
And it is in the returning
where the soul realizes its gain,
in the renewing light.

Contend

Loss triggers fear
because we cannot perceive
outside our limited senses.
What we do not know
or understand
is a threat to our own survival.
Belief is not knowledge or experience.
It is human to question
the nature of the soul—
the light that animates the human being,
the light that vanishes from human sight.
We forget who we are,
so we forget what happens
when we leave.
We assume an end of existence
from our perspective of mortality—
this is the human condition.
It is ours with which to struggle,
with which to contend,
to reconcile in our own hearts.
And what we sense of light and life,
in others and in ourselves,
is if light continues, life continues,
for light is life
and exists whether in or apart from flesh.

Uncertain Air

Beyond this darkness,
a great light radiates glory,
though you cannot see it now.
In the midst of life,
you lost sight of what you once knew,
longing to experience it again,
though not knowing how
or why.
It is a song you hum
but cannot remember the words.
It is the face you faintly recognize
but cannot remember the name.
Then the thought vanishes.
In time, you will remember.
To live is the greatest accomplishment of all.
To dare to breathe
uncertain air
is the greatest risk you could take,
accepting the journey
where everything is at stake
though nothing is promised.
But you may glimpse the great light
when autumn turns the leaves from green to gold,
when winter paints the earth with silver light,
when spring brings hope and purpose to the world.

Surviving

This difficulty will pass,
as all things must pass,
here in a temporary world
where experience brings a permanent impact
on the soul.
You struggled with understanding
such a heavy loss,
the world leaving you empty
with its silence.
But silence is how it communicates
its most important lessons.
This world is not for answering all your questions,
but for giving the cause to ask,
that you may endeavor to seek,
and perhaps find,
though the purpose is not the answer.
Though all life you may remember the pain,
you will also remember
how you coped,
how you struggled but never gave up,
how you walked again
when you thought you could not go on,
how you moved forward
through impenetrable darkness

only to emerge
with the light of life in your hand.
The accomplishment of life
is the struggle to survive.

Willing

Just take a step.
You do not have to have the answer,
but the willingness to look.
If some pain of sorrow or loss
is too much,
you can still open your eyes.
You do not need to remain
in the dark fear of beginning again.
In beginning again,
you do not leave behind what you lost,
for nothing is ever truly lost,
but remains part of you.
Moving on is not a cutting off
of what helped make you who you are,
but an incorporation in a new direction
of all you loved.
Each new moment is a gift
that brings healing to the soul,
the lessening of even the worst grief,
as you move toward welcoming light,
the renewal of the path
on this journey of self-discovery.

Visible

You feared the dark time
because you did not know
what lived there.
Loss led you by the hand
against your will
through the gate of the unknown.
In the blackness,
apparitions appeared and disappeared—
the ghosts that hovered all life out of sight.
The darkness made them visible,
so you could finally see them
for what they were.
And then you knew the boundary of fear,
that it can only go so far,
and so deep.
The journey inward
was a gift you could not acknowledge
until on the way out.
The insight you gained
was the expansion you wanted,
the movement of perfecting the soul.

Endure

Let today be the last day
you hold on to fear.
Why not look forward
to what could be possible?
Frustration is only temporary,
unless you stop trying,
for then you allow it to remain.
But you have greater things to discover,
to uncover,
a path to walk
that leads somewhere brighter,
a place you know
but perhaps lost sight of.
Every heart falters from time to time,
for this is the way of the human,
always moving through high and low
as it journeys forward,
its destiny unfolding step by step
until it reaches the threshold
of why it lives—
something about a horizon,
or a golden light,
or a place where memories return
that proves the accomplishment
of overcoming what it feared.

Anticipation

We prepare ourselves for grief
before it arrives,
in the hope we can better handle
the afterwards.
We want to know
where the path leads
before we travel it.
Thoughts press forward
to envision what loss feels like—
What kind of pain is it?
Will I be lonely?
What is the depth of sorrow?
We haunt ourselves with future ghosts
that have not yet appeared,
in the hope
we will recognize them in the dark,
to dispel fear,
to remove surprise,
to lessen the impact.
Darkness is a momentary pause
that must give way to light,
and human nature,
in the foresight of anticipation,
senses, feels, expects, forecasts,
for such a passing through.

Pathway

You thought no coming back
was possible.
The loss was too severe—
a darkness you could not see through,
unable to discern the path ahead.
Where would you go?
How would you feel?
Could you stand again
and engage the world with confidence,
with sincerity,
with love?
What will happen in the afterwards?
Uncertainty is not impossibility.
Take the time you need.
The heart knows how to heal
and will move again when it is ready.
Then you will stand,
and each step you take
will create a new way forward.
The path will show itself to you,
unfolding purpose,
providing meaning,
revealing promise for the time to come.
Uncertainty will fade along with the pain,

and you will embrace living,
feeling warmth again,
love again,
life again.

Shine

Lift your head
even when you feel you can't,
for you might see something
that changes your perspective.
Although the ocean expanse
and mountain valley
are breathtaking,
the inspiration of life
is also in the falling leaf,
the swaying grass,
and the butterfly that can't hold still
long enough for you to see its colors.
Such a sight can lift the darkness
that smothers hope and peace.
So, look, and live.
For what is life,
that you should not shine with it?
It is yours to have,
it is for you,
it is you.

Reap

Move now
before the moment passes,
before you lose the chance
to do what you intended.
Do not let fear of unrealized potential
hold you back.
If you could remember your origin,
you would laugh at such hesitation,
knowing that the reward
is not in the accomplishment,
but in the attempt.
The time for celebrating your achievements
is a far-off light on the horizon,
whose time will come
when you reach your destination.
Nothing is forgotten.
The light will remember everything you
said,
did,
and felt,
and the struggle you accepted
with the full risk of losing,
though nothing is really lost.
Move now,

so you may reap the treasure of trial,
always becoming,
ever changing,
ever overcoming.

Momentary

Press forward in difficulty.
You will get through.
Nothing is permanent,
not even the obstacle
that impedes your progress.
The struggle is momentary
against the background of the infinite glow.
The great light never ceases to exist,
for its nature is life,
so it must live,
whether you can see it or not.
So, you also must live,
for the light is your home,
and you are of the light.
Hardship is a momentary opponent
that always relents in the end,
as it must.
Take courage.
What trial can withstand the force of light?

Remain

Let the first light of morning
be to you a recall
of all you are
and from where you have come.
Light is never so welcome
as when it first appears.
It is both the onset of a new day
and the guide out of darkness.
To fear the dark is human,
for human nature fears
what it cannot see.
But darkness is never final.
The soul is made of light,
and its origin is light.
It slows only for a brief time
to understand itself
against the backdrop of a darker hue,
a purposed night,
a journey through the veil of separation,
that it may dim itself
enough to see its own outline,
to know itself in all potential forms.
You are never alone,
though sometimes you feel so.

You are purpose playing out,
intention fulfilling its desire,
light that overcomes,
that remains.

Symphony

Life continues.
What unfavorable condition
in yourself or another
caused you such grief?
It was the loss of potential moments,
the experience you wanted
but could not have.
So, you kept walking anyway,
not knowing where you were going,
but you were moving.
You took life as it came,
making the most of this or that,
although it never met your expectation.
Your ideal was higher than
what was actually possible.
It was not your fault.
Life is a symphony of chaos and form,
each trying to persuade the other
of its way forward.
And through such adversity, you lived,
for the point all along was to live.

Rise

Come back from where you have been.
You are never so far down
so as not to be able to come back up,
even though it may feel so.
Life is a never-ending ebb and flow
of pleasure and pain,
of struggle and victory.
Life reveals its purpose in the living,
in the experience of moments,
in the sadness of being overcome,
and in the joy of overcoming—
both are necessary attributes
of the nature of this world,
neither existing without the other.
We curse difficulty in all forms
because we think it is harmful,
but it is opportunity in disguise.
This world presents hardship to us
so that we may know ourselves
through the process of struggle.
Opposition challenges the soul
and brings about the glory of discovery,
like when you do not think you can stand again
after being down so long,

but you can,
and are here to do so,
to find yourself again amid discouragement,
to leave sorrow behind,
to come back from where you have been,
to rise to heights that you have not yet known.

Breathing

Such is the beauty of living,
that you willingly accepted
the inevitable casualty of heartache
to experience it.
Why should the beauty of living
require such a counterpart?
Because the soul longs
to give itself in full,
desiring to know completely,
to understand,
to be understood,
to commune.
The individuality of flesh
creates the necessity of choice,
to like or dislike,
to accept or deny,
to be drawn to or repelled.
Always the duality in everything here.
Choice creates the burden to find,
that the soul may reach its objective.
The state of permanence is impossible,
for nothing ever stays the same,
except for the searching and finding,
the loving and losing,
like the in and out of the tide,
or of breathing.

Favor

Do not forget to love.
Give grace to those
who do not deserve it.
Show warmth to those
that life has hardened.
Listen to those
who do not know what to say.
Grant patience to those
who stall in the difficulty to move.
See in others
the potential for good,
regardless of what past actions show.
Look for the positive in others,
when all they know is the negative.
Love gives others the favor to live.
Strive to overcome your limitations
as each situation gives opportunity,
a worthy endeavor,
for your time here is momentary,
until you return from where you came,
as all others will,
and the light will reflect back to you
all you accomplished,
the love you gave.

Midwinter

Time must pass
before you pick it up again.
Clarity comes through the distance
from where you began
to where you are now.
Looking back at the tracks in the snow
refreshes your memory
of the excitement you had in starting,
and renews hope
that you can finish what you intended.
Midwinter is the time for pause,
for reflection,
to recalibrate expectations,
and process the gain already accomplished.
The darkest days can give the grace of peace.
Do not fear the dimmed light,
but revel in the solitude of the season,
of standing still long enough
to observe your shadow on the frosted ground,
and of looking forward to the path ahead,
knowing that the snow
can only hide the way for a moment.

Live

Never give up.
You were born to move forward,
to continue,
even when the obstacle
looks insurmountable.
Fear reminds you
you are human,
that you can hurt.
But that is all it can do.
It does not have authority to hold you
down,
or keep you from accomplishing desire,
but disappears with a new perspective.
Live.
Imagine what is possible
and then grasp it.
All is within your reach,
if you would only hold out your hand.
You will find the way through,
gaining the wisdom trial brings,
learning the nature of striving and struggling
in the face of what you wanted
and what you doubted.

Reflection

The end is never the same
as the beginning.
When the world is new,
the light is a different hue
of gold,
but enough to remind you of home.
You forget how long it takes
to acclimate to this way of being,
moving in slow motion
with full sensation
through a world where illusion
weaves the fabric of reality.
You do not ponder
your coming and going
while living.
You will not remember
until you are standing
again in front of the open door of light,
unable yet to see through to the other side,
through this light at the end
that should blind you but doesn't.
It is here where you see yourself,
face to face,
your own eyes staring back at you,

a reflection in water whose
ripples are the passage of your life,
where it went and what it did,
who you loved,
and how you grew.
Then the façade will fade,
when you return
in the full splendor of self-awareness
of who you are
and have always been.

Yearning

The truth hid somewhere between
what you could not see
and what you suspected.
And yet again, dear Soul,
this is the human condition—
to yearn to understand
all that this slow light hides
in the guise of its brilliance,
never giving away the answer
though you ask again and again.
The mundane is a mask
that frustrates you
with its repetition,
that keeps you from glimpsing
what sits just behind its wall,
just beyond its manifestation,
that if you could finally see,
then you would know.
But this life is not for the knowing,
but for the doing,
where questions form and mark the forward path,
to give you growth and gain,
and lead you back again to the golden shore,
the place where you began,
the light that is your home.

Continuity

Life will never end.
You will endure
even through the final breath
that all life you feared.
There is no finality,
only passing through the veil
where memory returns.
You had to believe you were finite—
how else would you accomplish
such a glorious endeavor?
All will be disclosed in its time,
but not while you are here.
This world must fulfill its purpose
in being everything you needed,
even what scared you,
all you wanted but could not remember.
Dimming light is light
despite the lack of sight.
All will be recounted.
No true end exists,
only returning to
the light you left,
the light of your enduring life.

Individuated

The forever light of the golden shore
disappeared from your eyes
as you wept in the sadness and hope
of leaving.
Light in slow motion
was the promise of gain
through adversity.
It was the journey from completion
to distortion
and back again.
The distortion gave you opportunity
to see yourself differently,
to discover where and how to change.
The soul desires growth
so that it may discover itself,
for it is of the light which gave it birth.
But being one and yet individuated
is a contradiction
the soul yearns to understand,
so it fractures itself
into a million pieces of light,
that it may discover all its potential existence.
The great light is infinite,
the only true permanence that exists.
It is all that exists
and can ever exist.

Sacred

Far past the boundary
of physical sight,
the light cannot hide its essence,
for it is the source of everything,
and is in everything.
You cannot understand this while living.
The human mind can only fathom
its own limitation,
in light so slow
that it only sees its own form.
It cannot know what it does not experience.
Form is an illusion of the light—
the beauty of the universe
displayed in sacred patterns
that solidified into touch and sight,
and even yourself.
The remembrance of light
was never so strong
as when you first breathed in—
not a new existence,
but a different one,
one where density dictated function
and purpose,
your course set before your arrival,

to live and to love,
to want and be satisfied,
and to long and to lose.
Unknowing, you knew.
It was all for you,
all for you.

Wavelength

In the fall,
the light changes.
By then, you will have learned
everything you wanted
about the varying nature of light—
how it brightens and fades,
how it reflects and refracts,
how it shortens and lengthens
to display its full spectrum,
each color a different wavelength of experience.
You moved in fascination
of all your eye took in,
processing, incorporating,
acknowledging, accepting.
You tracked the sun
from equinox to solstice to equinox,
embracing the truth
that this is the way of the world,
that a time exists for rising and falling,
waxing and waning,
increasing and lessening.
But light is light regardless of its luminance.
And in this dimming light,
you look back with longing for

the love you gave and received,
and how it changed you
in your passing through.
Past traveling points you to your destination—
unknown and yet familiar.
Have you passed this way before?
The darkest night of the year is still to come.
But no real beginning or ending exists,
only the illusion of coming and going.

Light In Slow Motion

Light so slow that it densifies into form
was a contradiction you could not get over,
creating a world so foreign to your nature
yet somehow retaining its essence.
You watched the universe coalesce
from the vantage point of infinity,
considering desire
and if you had the fortitude to experience it.
The final result
was a world so beautiful and savage
that it shook you to your core.
This world was unique
in that it gave the opportunity
both to love and to lose,
to embrace and to weep.
It did not promise safety and security,
but allowed for anything to happen—
a masterpiece of potential
presenting good and bad,
the glorious and the terrible,
where the only true comfort
was in the light of another,
though you could not see it,
but perhaps could recognize it.

The reality of loss
is non-existent in the golden realm,
for only life exists there.
But the soul searches for growth
through the newness of experience,
to do what it has not done before,
to become what it has not yet become,
to know what it otherwise cannot know.
This world provided the chance
to know the pain of detachment,
disconnection,
estrangement,
and to say goodbye.
Loss would be the greatest teacher,
for it requires acceptance
of what you cannot control,
and forces you to try to reconcile
what is perceivably unreconcilable
while blind in flesh.
It is not until you awaken
that you may contemplate what is divine.
This world required a separation
from all memory of the golden realm—
so that you could have the opportunity
to discover your own self as if for the first time,
as when your light first came forth,
the nuance of your soul,
that, while one with the light,
is distinguished by its own hue and personhood.

This life would embed the totality
of all you are,
then hide it from you
so as not to hinder the journey
of becoming self-aware,
a slow remembering,
learning through self-discovery,
trying, failing, searching, growing—
the golden gain of finding light again,
in others and in yourself.
The physical nature of this world
provided the necessary means
to conceal the essence of the light,
something impossible yet possible
through a slower vibratory frequency
collapsing in a downward spiral,
creating the illusion of touch,
of heaviness, pressure, and pain,
and perhaps its foremost achievement—
fear.
No true separation exists,
except for what you make yourself believe.
Without separation,
there is no fear,
for fear requires the potential for harm.
Fear cannot exist in the golden realm,
for all is one,
and nothing exists except for the one,
and the one can only bring forth from itself,

for it is all that exists.
Fear is the illusion of separation
from the one,
a momentary descent into form
so dense it convinces you
that you are alone, lost, forsaken.
And it is here where your journey begins,
loving, leaving, losing, learning, lamenting,
striving to understand who you are
and how at times the world could be so cruel,
the veil so thick
you believe nothing more exists.
The silence of God
would be the hardest part to bear,
for no answer would be provided
despite the yearning, the crying out,
and the pleading.
But the answer as to the why of things
is not the final destination;
purpose and reason unfold through experience,
only revealing themselves in full
upon your return,
your final destination,
the golden realm of light
where nothing ever fades,
your descent from
the light of who you are,
and ascent back to
the light from where you came,

your home.
This world is beautiful,
offering both tragedy and triumph,
the gift of knowing and expanding.
You are forever loved
despite what happens in the flesh.
Nothing is ever lost,
but is incorporated into the light.
And so, there you stood,
on the edge of the golden shore,
looking out far enough
to where gold fades to black,
the horizon of hope and expectation,
the wondrous unknown,
your feet ready to step out,
to endeavor,
this opportunity to discover,
to embrace this dream of life,
this light in slow motion.

Thematic Subject Index

The poems in this book contain a variety of themes. Sometimes, a single poem will touch on multiple themes. The following subject index lists out some of the more major themes and highlights where they are more prominently featured.

About the Author

Keith Wrassmann holds the degrees of MA in Creative Writing: Poetry from Miami University (Oxford, OH) and MDiv in Theology from Cincinnati Christian University, where he also won the Theological Studies Award. He lives in the greater Cincinnati, Ohio area with his wife and children.

Visit www.keithwrassmann.com for more.

9 7 8 1 9 6 1 6 3 1 0 3 8